ADVENTURES WITH ART

D1520115

ADVENTURES WITH ART

Concept-Based Art Projects

Sarah Jenkins
Margaret Foote

Illustrated by Sarah Jenkins

GoodYearBooks

An Imprint of ScottForesman
A Division of HarperCollinsPublishers

Dedicated to all the Violets in the world who inspire us . . .

Cover art contributors:
Anna and Michael Doherty
Jenna Halvorsen
Elaine and Sarah McKenna

GoodYearBooks
are available for most basic curriculum subjects plus many
enrichment areas. For more GoodYearBooks, contact your local
bookseller or educational dealer. For a complete catalog with
information about other GoodYearBooks, please write:

GoodYearBooks
ScottForesman
1900 East Lake Avenue
Glenview, IL 60025

Book Design by Matthew Doherty Design.
Copyright © 1993 Sarah Jenkins and Margaret Foote.
All Rights Reserved.
Printed in the United States of America.

ISBN 0-673-46415-6

5 6 7 8 9 – EQ – 01 00 99 98

Preface

We created *Adventures with Art* because we felt a need for a book of art activities that required a minimum of materials and little preparation, generated excitement, and taught the basic concepts of art—activities that would stimulate the creative abilities of children and look terrific upon completion!

As we taught elementary art in the past fifteen years, we began to keep files of projects categorized according to seasons and concepts. We felt that others who work with children might be able to benefit from our experiences and what had worked well for us. Eventually we decided to compile these ideas into a book.

As we developed our book idea, the character of "Art" emerged. He has become not only our main character but our friend. We hope you enjoy the book as Art takes you on some of his adventures.

Sarah Jenkins
Margaret Foote

Contents, by Season

Contents, by Concept

From *Adventures with Art*, published by GoodYearBooks. Copyright © 1993 Sarah Jenkins and Margaret Foote.

Contents, by Skill Level

From *Adventures with Art*, published by GoodYearBooks. Copyright © 1993 Sarah Jenkins and Margaret Foote.

Introduction

The elementary school years are a prime time for adults to encourage and nurture creativity and a love for art in children. It is during this time that a child's artistic confidence is either built or suppressed. *Adventures with Art*'s activities focus on building that confidence. They are easy to understand, require a minimum of materials, and generate excitement about art.

The activities also focus on teaching art concepts. It is important to know and understand that an artist uses these concepts individually, as well as together, to create a pleasing work of art. As a student has several experiences working with each concept, he or she will gain confidence and begin to use them in his or her own projects.

The projects in this book work well with children in grades 1-6. Teachers and parents can present them to groups of children or use them with individual children. In addition, *Adventures with Art* can also be used by teenagers and adults as a self-teaching tool.

The book is divided into three sections: projects for **Fall**, for **Winter**, and for **Spring**. Each activity includes an appropriate skill level and the main concept it teaches, along with related concepts. We've included three tables of contents—by season, by skill level, and by main concept—allowing you to reference all of the projects in a particular category.

The skill levels give you an approximate guide to the appropriateness of an activity for your group:

Easy: Grades 1 and 2 (Ages 6 to 8)
Intermediate: Grades 3 and 4 (Ages 8 to 10)
Advanced: Grades 5 and 6 (Ages 10 to 12)

You can adapt activities to a different level, and we have provided suggestions at the end of most of the projects to help you do just that.

The order in which you use the activities is up to you. You may choose to teach all activities for one concept successively, regardless of season, or you may want to present the activities in their indicated seasons, reinforcing a concept at different times throughout the year.

The activities are easy to understand and present. You'll need approximately 15 to 20 minutes to explain the directions. The actual time needed for an activity will vary according to the project. Most can be completed within a one-hour art period. You'll also find that the materials needed for the activities are readily accessible. The paper sizes are standard, and the other needed materials are found in most school supply rooms or stores.

It is a good idea to make an example of the project as you discuss the directions with the children; this will give them a visual reference as they make their own projects. However, remind students that they shouldn't simply copy your project. The true joy of art is in the creation of something new and different. Ask students to interpret the project each in his or her own way.

Above all, don't give students dittoed work to color; let them express their creativity by starting with blank paper and a pencil. Occasionally a basic pattern is useful, but only for the beginnings of a picture, never for an entire project. If a student copies or just colors, the work is no longer his or her own. Be sure to praise every student, for each piece will have in it something that will delight. Your praise will build their confidence and give them the desire to draw and create again and again.

To reinforce that confidence, it is important to display students' work as often as possible. When you display the finished products, use paper, posterboard, or something creative to make a frame or border around the picture. This can be simply glued or stapled. It will make the picture look nicer and create a beautiful display. It willalso give the artist a sense of pride in his or her work.

Last, but certainly not least, we have given life to a character named, appropriately, "Art." You'll find Art on many pages in this book. He is there to add fun and humor to each project. Art will entertain your students, and, we hope, inspire them as he has us.

From *Adventures with Art*, published by GoodYearBooks. Copyright © 1993 Sarah Jenkins and Margaret Foote.

The Concepts

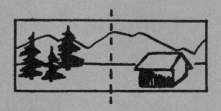

Balance

The term "balance" refers to the arrangement of all parts of an artwork to create a sense of equality on all sides. The weight or size of objects, their placement, and their color must all be balanced in a work of art. There are three types of balance: symmetrical, asymmetrical, and radial.

Symmetrical Balance

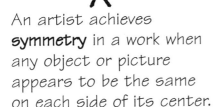

An artist achieves **symmetry** in a work when any object or picture appears to be the same on each side of its center.

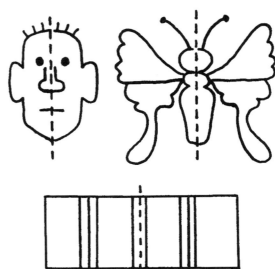

Asymmetrical Balance

An **asymmetrical** arrangement has two sides that are not exactly alike but the overall effect is one of balance.

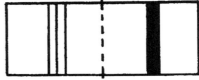

Radial Balance

An artwork has **radial** balance if the elements of the work branch out in all directions from a common point.

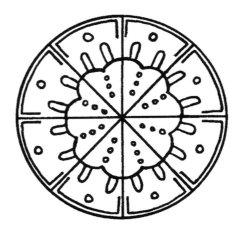

Color

When talking about color, we use the terms "hue," "value," and "brightness."

Hue refers to the six true colors: red, orange, yellow, green, blue, and violet. These are the primary and secondary colors you find on a color wheel such as the one below.

Value refers to how light or dark the color is.

Brightness refers to the intensity of a color: How bright or dull is that color?

Primary Colors

The three **primary colors** are red, yellow, and blue. They are called "primary" because you can't mix any other colors to make these, but you can use these colors in different combinations to make other colors.

Secondary Colors

Secondary colors are made by mixing two primary colors: Red and Blue make Violet. Red and Yellow make Orange. Blue and Yellow make Green.

This color wheel shows how to mix primary colors to make secondary colors. The arrangement of the colors on the wheel show the sequential relationship between the colors as you move around the wheel.

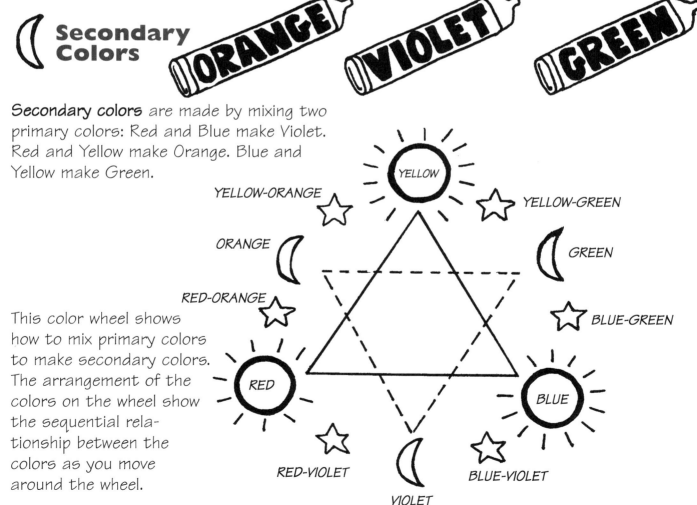

From *Adventures with Art*, published by GoodYearBooks. Copyright © 1993 Sarah Jenkins and Margaret Foote.

Complementary Colors

Complementary colors are two colors that are opposite on a color wheel, such as red and green. They are placed opposite because they do not share any basic (primary) colors.

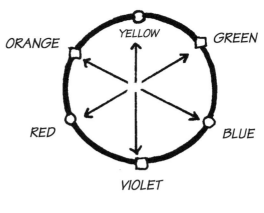

Analogous Colors

Analogous colors are three or four colors that are adjacent (next to each other) on a color wheel, such as yellow, yellow-orange, and orange. Analogous colors create a harmonious effect.

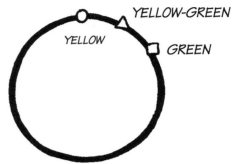

Monochromatic Color Scheme

You can make a **tint** by adding white to a color. You can make a **shade** by adding black to a color. A **monochromatic** color scheme includes one color and its tints and shades.

When you add white to a hue, you achieve a tint. For example, pink is a tint of red, because when you add red and white you get pink. When you add black to a hue, you achieve a shade. Navy blue is a shade of blue, made by adding black to blue.

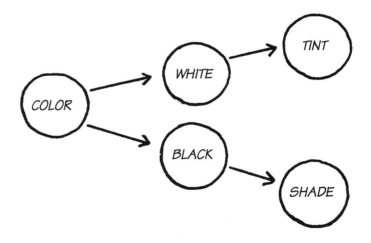

Color Value

We use this term to refer to the lightness or darkness of a color. This includes all the shades in between.

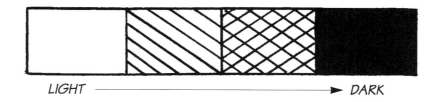

LIGHT ⟶ DARK

Color Intensity

This term refers to the brightness or dullness of a color. Brightness refers to a color in its most vivid degree. A **bright** color seems to jump out at you. **Dullness** refers to the color at its weakest or softest degree. Dull colors are more subtle than bright ones. Dull colors are made by mixing a color and its complement (its opposite on the color wheel). For example, you can make blue dull by adding orange to it.

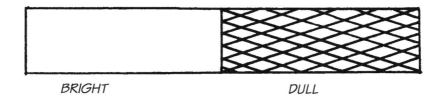

BRIGHT DULL

Mood

We use art to create a **mood**, stimulating emotion in the person who is viewing the piece of art. We use color to create a mood. Look at the illustration at the right. Half of the colors on the wheel are "warm" colors, and the other half are "cool." These help us create a mood with art.

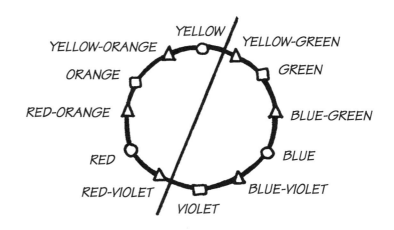

Design

We use the terms **design** or **composition** to refer to the arrangement of lines, forms, colors, and textures in an artwork. A good design shows an orderly arrange-ment of the materials used, and, in addition, creates beauty in the finished product. Design is broken down into smaller concepts: space, proportion, variety, repetition, emphasis, contrast, light, and style.

Space

Space is the three-dimensional expanse in which living and inanimate objects exist. It is also the term used to refer to the distance or interval between objects. In art, space is the illusion of distance. This distance includes the background, horizon line, and foreground in a picture.

The Horizon Line is at the viewer's eye level, where the sky and ground in the picture seem to meet. Avoid drawing the horizon line exactly in the middle of the picture. Lines and objects should always be placed "off center" to avoid cutting the picture in half.

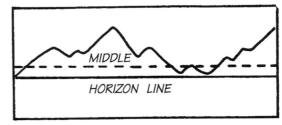

The Background of a picture refers to objects or shapes that appear in the distance. These objects enhance the picture but are not the main focus of attention.

The Foreground refers to objects or shapes that are the main focus of attention and appear closest to the viewer of the picture. These are the largest objects in the picture, located on the lower half of the page, giving the effect of nearness.

Proportion

The relationship of size, colors, and shapes to each other and within the picture as a whole is called **proportion.** For example, an artist tries to show the right proportion between a head and a body, or a nose on a face, in a picture.

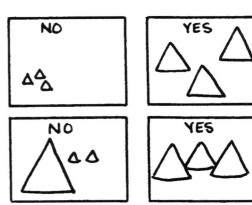

From *Adventures with Art*, published by GoodYearBooks. Copyright © 1993 Sarah Jenkins and Margaret Foote.

Variety

Variety refers to the use of a diversity of materials and techniques in an artwork. This is necessary in order for the design to be interesting.

Repetition

By repeating elements such as colors, lines, and shapes in an artwork, you create visual interest. A picture is said to have **unity** if all elements are in harmony so that the finished product has a sense of "wholeness." If the elements don't work together, the artwork will give a viewer a sense of **confusion.**

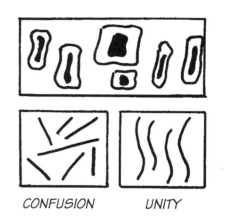

CONFUSION   UNITY

Emphasis

The **emphasis** of an artwork is the point of the viewer's focus. The emphasis is determined by the size, color value, and dominance of an object or shape in the artwork.

Contrast

This term refers to the differences of color shapes, and textures within an artwork. Are the textures rough or smooth? Are the colors dark or light? The edge where dark and light meet creates the **contour** of the shape in the work.

Light

As you look at a picture, where is the light in the picture coming from? Make sure that shadows in the picture fall away from the direction of the light source. Light includes its own vocabulary:

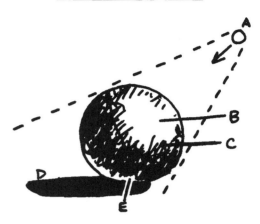

Light Source (A)

The direction from which the light comes in the picture.

Highlight (B)

The place on the object that is exposed fully to the light source—where the light hits the object directly.

Halftone (C)

The soft edge of the light where it meets shadow, or a gradual transition from light to dark.

Shadow (D)

This is the dark area on an artwork where the light is blocked out, just like your own shadow.

Reflected Light (E)

The lightened area in a shadow created by light bouncing off another object. This causes portions of the shadow to be lightened slightly.

Style

The manner in which a picture is put together is called **style**. Is the style realistic, meaning that the picture paints the world as it actually appears? Or is it abstract, meaning that the picture works as a design but is not true to life?

From *Adventures with Art*, published by GoodYearBooks. Copyright © 1993 Sarah Jenkins and Margaret Foote.

Line

Line is the simplest, most primitive, and universal means for creating visual art. Lines can be straight, such as those that are horizontal, vertical, or diagonal; or lines can be curved, showing action, life, and energy. Lines can be enhanced by the degree of thickness, sharpness of angles, and the depth of their value (lightness or darkness).

Types of Lines

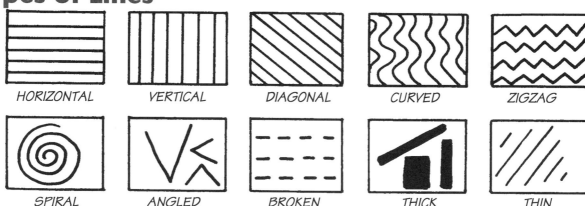

Rhythm

Rhythm is related to movement, which is created by lines showing energy. The rhythm of an artwork involves the regular repetition of lines, shapes, colors, and patterns. It is the easy path of lines, forms, or colors along which the viewer's eye travels as he or she looks at the artwork.

Types of Rhythm

REPETITION
FORMS
PATTERNS

PROCESSION OF
SIZES—SMALL
TO LARGE OR
VICE VERSA

CONTINUOUS
LINE MOVEMENT

ALTERNATING
LINES

THIN TO THICK

Enhancing Lines

Lines which give more detail or create a three-dimensional effect are called **enhancing lines**. These are used for shading or giving depth to an object.

SHADING

CROSSHATCHING

From *Adventures with Art*, published by GoodYearBooks. Copyright © 1993 Sarah Jenkins and Margaret Foote.

Perspective

The term **perspective** refers to the technique for making a flat, or one-dimensional, picture appear to have depth. Using the principles on this page, an artist can give an artwork the effect of distance, or perspective.

Types of Perspective

High-Low

Objects that are lower in the picture appear closer to the viewer, while objects that are high appear further away.

Large-Small

Large objects appear closer to the viewer, but small objects appear further away.

Overlapping

The technique of overlapping allows an artist to create the illusion of depth. Objects that appear in front of other objects appear closer to the viewer, while objects that are behind appear further away.

Dark-Light

Dark objects appear closer while light objects appear further away from the viewer.

Detail

When you move away from an object, you can see less of its detail. In an artwork, then, use less detail on objects in the background and more detail on objects in the foreground.

From *Adventures with Art*, published by GoodYearBooks. Copyright © 1993 Sarah Jenkins and Margaret Foote.

Shapes

A line drawn to enclose an area forms a **shape**. Shapes can be geometric or free form, and they can be contoured, positive, or negative within an artwork.

Types of Shapes

Geometric

Basic mathematical shapes, such as squares and triangles. These shapes can be flat, such as a circle, triangle, or square, or three-dimensional, such as cubes, spheres, and cones.

Free Form

  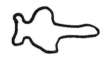

Forms that have no distinct or definite shape. These can be creative, irregularly shaped, and free-flowing.

Contour

The basic outline or edge of any given object.

Positive and Negative

Positive shapes in a picture are those that are the main focus of the picture, while negative shapes are those that are less noticeable. Both are necessary to the complete picture.

POSITIVE   NEGATIVE

There are three rules to drawing shapes:

1. Draw large shapes first, then draw the smaller, detailed shapes.
2. Use shadows, highlights, and reflections to enhance the shapes in a picture.
3. Add texture and shading to show form. In an artwork, form refers to the three-dimensional characteristics of an object.

From *Adventures with Art*, published by GoodYearBooks. Copyright © 1993 Sarah Jenkins and Margaret Foote.

Texture

The term **texture** refers to the surface of an object or artwork—how it looks and how it feels. In art, texture is represented by creating a rough or smooth surface effect. This can be achieved by the use of repetition, spattering, rubbing, or daubing techniques.

Achieving Textural Effects

Repetition

Create a pattern in an artwork by repeating a line or a shape. The pattern becomes a textural effect.

Spattering

By spattering paint on the artwork with a toothbrush, paintbrush, or spray can, you can add specks or dots, which can become shapes.

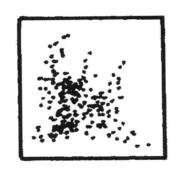 

Rubbing

Place the artwork on a textured surface, such as a large rock. Using a pencil or crayon, rub over the paper until you have created the rock's surface on the paper.

Daubing

Using a sponge or wad of paper soaked with paint, spot a piece of paper or an object, creating a painted effect.

From Adventures with Art, published by GoodYearBooks. Copyright © 1993 Sarah Jenkins and Margaret Foote.

Fall

The adventure begins, today is the day,
Follow Art as he makes his way
Through pencils, paper, scissors, and glue.
Art experiences await you!

The way to start is to jump right in,
Art will show you how to begin.
Hues are bright, leaves are turning,
And while you have fun, you'll be learning.

Birds of a Feather

Materials

Each Child Needs:
- ○ 9" x 12" piece of black construction paper
- ○ bird body pattern
- ○ assorted pieces of colored construction paper
- ○ scissors
- ○ glue
- ○ pictures of different birds

Advanced

CONCEPTS

Perspective Color

Directions

Before getting started, discuss with the children bird types, color variations, and feather shapes. Show them the bird pictures.

Then, have the children:

1. Select the type of bird they would like to create and decide on the colors they will need.

2. Cut out the bird body pattern and glue it to the center of the black paper.

3. Real feathers come in different lengths, widths, and textures. When cutting out feathers, cut them in clumps or groups (not individually) according to their location on the body. To do so, draw one of each size feather to use as a pattern. Place the patterns on top of the folded paper. Cut out the pattern through all layers of the paper, producing several feathers at once. Repeat this for each feather pattern you've created.

From *Adventures with Art*, published by GoodYearBooks. Copyright © 1993 Sarah Jenkins and Margaret Foote.

BACK

WING

HEAD

BREAST

16
FALL

On the back of a bird, Art takes flight,

4. Arrange the feathers on the body pattern beginning with the tail feathers and working to the head. All feathers should be pointing in the same direction, with the head, wing, and tail feathers overlapping the others.

5. Cut out a leg, an eye, and a beak. Add a speck of white to each eye with a small piece of white paper or with a white crayon. Attach these parts to the birds.

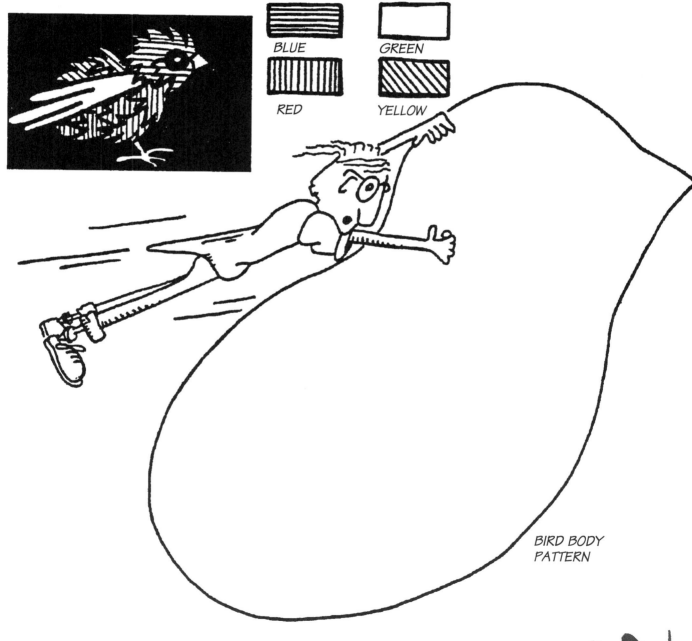

BLUE

GREEN

RED

YELLOW

BIRD BODY PATTERN

He's holding on with all his might.

Designer Names

Materials

Each Child Needs:
- ⭘ 12" x 18" piece of construction paper
- ⭘ pencil
- ⭘ crayons
- ⭘ scissors
- ⭘ black marker

Easy

CONCEPTS

Design Texture

Directions

Before getting started, write each child's name on a piece of art paper with the marker. Use large, open letters, and position the letters so that their outlines touch.

Then have the children:

1. Draw a design inside each letter with a pencil. Draw different designs and color in each darkly.

2. Cut out his or her entire name. Display the names on the bulletin board.

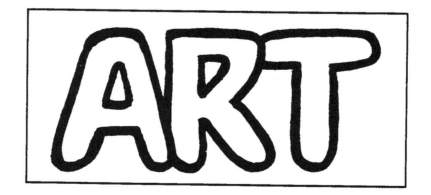

Weary and tired, Art needs some rest.

Suggestions

1. Children can design each letter to represent one of their own hobbies or characteristics.

2. To extend this activity, have each child draw a shoe, whatever type the child feels fits his or her personality—for example, a tennis shoe, dance slipper, or cowboy boot. Ask the children to design their shoes showing their own interests.

Tomorrow he'll go on and continue his quest.

Moving Models

Materials

Each Child Needs:
- ○ 9" x 9" piece of oaktag
- ○ 9" x 12" piece of white drawing paper
- ○ scissors
- ○ pencil
- ○ crayons

Intermediate

CONCEPTS

Line
Texture

Directions

Before getting started, discuss with the children how objects show movement. Movement is created in an artwork through the use of curved and bent lines; straight lines do not show energy. Some examples of movement in art include images of people or animals running, cars moving on a road, or birds flying.

Now, have the children:

1. On the oaktag, draw the outline of a simple object in motion (cars, people, animals). The object should be as large as the oaktag (1).

2. Cut out the shapes. The outside section becomes the stencil for a pattern.

3. Matching the top and bottom of the oaktag and white paper, place the pattern at the left margin (2).

4. Trace the inside of the pattern with a yellow crayon.

5. Move the pattern about 1/4-inch to the right. Trace the inside of the pattern with a yellow-orange crayon.

1

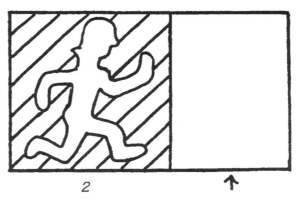

2

↑
WHITE PAPER

Faster, Art, pick up your pace,

From *Adventures with Art*, published by GoodYearBooks. Copyright © 1993 Sarah Jenkins and Margaret Foote.

6. Repeat the pattern every 1/4 inch using the following colors, in this order: orange, yellow-orange, green, blue-green, blue, red-violet, and black. Progress from light to dark colors. Use black as the final color. This should be the heaviest line in the design.

Suggestions

1. Give the picture a border by mounting the picture on a piece of slightly larger colored paper. The excess paper around the picture creates a natural border.

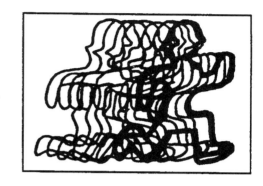

2. Color each design darkly.

3. Keep the top and bottom edges even every time you move the stencil. This will keep the picture in alignment.

Otherwise, you'll lose this race.

Scribble Art

Materials

Each Child Needs:
- ○ 12" x 18" piece of manila or white drawing paper
- ○ pencil
- ○ crayons
- ○ black marker
- ○ ruler

Easy

CONCEPTS

Design Line

Directions

Have the children:

1. Draw a border around the piece of art paper, one inch from the edge on all sides (1).

2. Draw a scribble design inside the border, covering most of the paper (2).

3. Using analogous colors, fill in the spaces between the lines. Color darkly (3).

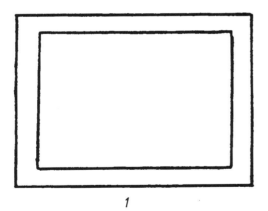

1

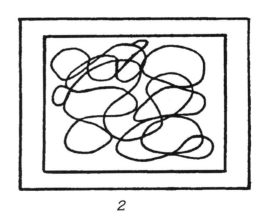

2

4. Older children: Outline the design and border with black marker. Younger children: Outline the children's designs for them.

This ferocious beast got out of his cage,

From Adventures with Art, published by GoodYearBooks. Copyright © 1993 Sarah Jenkins and Margaret Foote.

Suggestions

1. Have the children find and color an object in the design (4).

2. On a piece of white art paper, pre-draw a scribble design (you can do more than one design, but each paper should have a different design) (5). Have children study the design(s) at all angles, and then draw the pictures they see. Ask them to color their designs (6).

3. Have the children place 25 dots randomly on the paper. They can then connect the dots and see what object appears. Ask them to color the designs (7).

3

4

5

6

7

So Art escaped to the very next page.

Time in a Bottle

Materials

Each Child Needs:
- ○ 9" x 12" piece of orange construction paper
- ○ 5" x 7" piece of black construction paper
- ○ 3" x 8" piece of blue construction paper
- ○ white crayon
- ○ scissors
- ○ glue

Intermediate

CONCEPTS

**Perspective
Overlapping**

Directions

Before getting started, display examples of ships (sailing vessels of the 1700s and 1800s are preferable) for the children to see.

Then, have the children:

1. Fold the piece of orange paper in half. Draw half of a bottle on the fold of the orange paper. Make it as large as the paper (1).

2. Cut out the bottle.

3. Look at the examples of ships displayed in the classroom. On the black construction paper, draw and then cut out a silhouette of a ship (2).

4. Take the blue construction paper, and tear two waves (3).

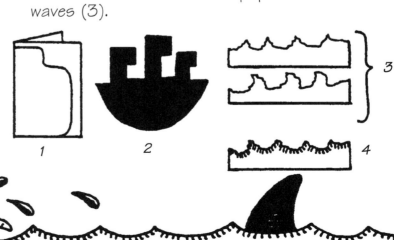

1   2   3   4

24
FALL

Safe at last, or so it seems,

From *Adventures with Art*, published by GoodYearBooks. Copyright © 1993 Sarah Jenkins and Margaret Foote.

5. With a white crayon, lightly color the top edge of the waves (4).

6. Place the ship between the two waves, and glue the ship and waves on the orange bottle (5).

7. Cut out 3 V-shaped birds, like seagulls, and glue them on the scene (5).

8. Used strips of white paper to decorate the neck of the bottle (6).

5

6

Suggestions

For a different effect, have the children try this:

1. On a 9" x 12" piece of white paper, do a watercolor wash using yellow, red, and orange paint. To do this, simply brush on a single layer of watercolor paint. Cover the entire page.

2. Do a similar wash on another piece of white paper. Use a combination of blue, green, and purple paint.

3. After the washes have dried, tear the blue wash into rows of waves. (Have the colored side facing you as you tear so you can get the "white cap" effect.)

4. Use the yellow wash for the background and sky. Use the blue for the water. Cut out the ship from black paper and place it between two waves.

5. Add birds with a marker or black paper (7).

7

 WATERCOLOR WASH (BLUE, RED, PURPLE)

 WATERCOLOR WASH (YELLOW, RED, ORANGE)

 BLACK CONSTRUCTION PAPER

Art's about to realize his worst dreams.

From *Adventures with Art*, published by GoodYearBooks. Copyright © 1993 Sarah Jenkins and Margaret Foote.

Cobweb Creatures

Materials

Each Child Needs:
- ⭘ pencil
- ⭘ scissors
- ⭘ 9" x 12" piece of black construction paper
- ⭘ 9" x 12" pieces of tissue paper in assorted colors
- ⭘ glue

Intermediate

CONCEPTS

**Balance
Line
Design**

Directions

Have the children:

1. Fold the black paper in half. Draw a one-inch border on three sides (1). Do not put a border on the fold.

2. On the fold, draw half of a creature (2). Sketch web lines, like a spider web, from the creature to the border (3). Draw the web lines as double lines.

3. With the paper folded, cut out the spaces between the webs (4). Cut through both sides of the folded paper, but don't cut through the border.

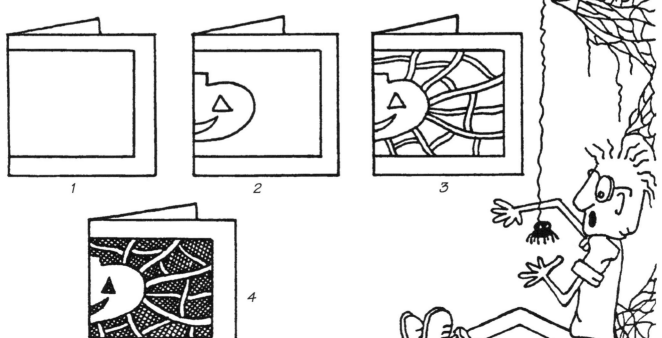

1

2

3

4

From *Adventures with Art*, published by GoodYearBooks. Copyright © 1993 Sarah Jenkins and Margaret Foote.

Awake from your dream, get up on your feet,

4. Unfold the black paper and glue a piece of tissue paper to the back (5 and 6). Trim around the outside edge to make a nicely finished picture. Display your creatures in your classroom.

5

6

Suggestions

This art project is great for Halloween, but it can also be used for other holidays.

There are many more people and creatures to meet.

Eerie Images
(Double Illusion)

Intermediate
CONCEPTS
Design Shape

Materials

Each Child Needs:
- one 9" x 18" piece of construction paper
- two 9" x 9" pieces of white drawing paper
- crayons
- pencil
- glue
- paper cutter

Directions

Before getting started, give each child two pieces of the white art paper.

Then, have the children:

1. Draw two objects, one on each piece of the 9" x 9" paper. Make the objects large and simple. Color the background one color without any detail (1). Color darkly.

 *1*

2. Ask an adult to place the pictures together. Then ask the adult to cut the pictures in one-inch strips using the paper cutter.

3. Assemble both pictures in this order (2):

1 2 3 4 5 6 7 8 9

2

1 2 3 4 5 6 7 8 9

28 FALL

Being folded and cut is not easy to do,

From *Adventures with Art*, published by GoodYearBooks. Copyright © 1993 Sarah Jenkins and Margaret Foote.

4. On the 9" x 18" paper, arrange the pictures in this pattern (3):

1 1 2 2 3 4 4 5 5 6 6 7 7 8 8 9 9

3

5. Glue the pieces to the larger paper, in order. Make sure the edges are close together and even (3).

6. Once dry, fold the big picture like a fan, with each picture piece becoming a different panel of the fan.

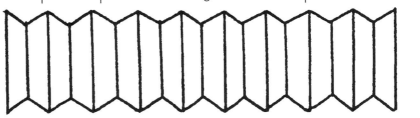

4

7. Look one way and see one picture. Turn the paper slightly sideways, and see the other picture.

Suggestions

This project is great for holiday images.

But if you're not careful it could happen to you.

Leafy Overlaps

Materials

Each Child Needs:
- ○ 9" x 12" piece of white drawing paper
- ○ 4 analogous-colored crayons
- ○ 3 leaf patterns
- ○ black crayon
- ○ ruler
- ○ pencil

Intermediate

CONCEPTS

Perspective
Color
Balance
Texture

Directions

Before getting started, review overlapping techniques with the children. Give each child a piece of white drawing paper.

Then, have the children:

1. Draw a one-inch border around the outside of the paper.

2. Select one of the leaf patterns.

3. Using a pencil, trace the leaves in an overlapping arrangement of five or seven leaves (1).

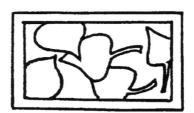

4. Take the darkest analogous color and do a vertical stroke around the edge of the first leaf. Color darkly—no white should show (2).

5. Repeat that stroke, going from darkest to lightest (3). Fill the space in the middle of the leaf with the lightest analogous color or leave it white.

The colors of fall keep Art spellbound,

From *Adventures with Art*, published by GoodYearBooks. Copyright © 1993 Sarah Jenkins and Margaret Foote.

6. After coloring all of the leaves, fill in the remaining background space with black (4).

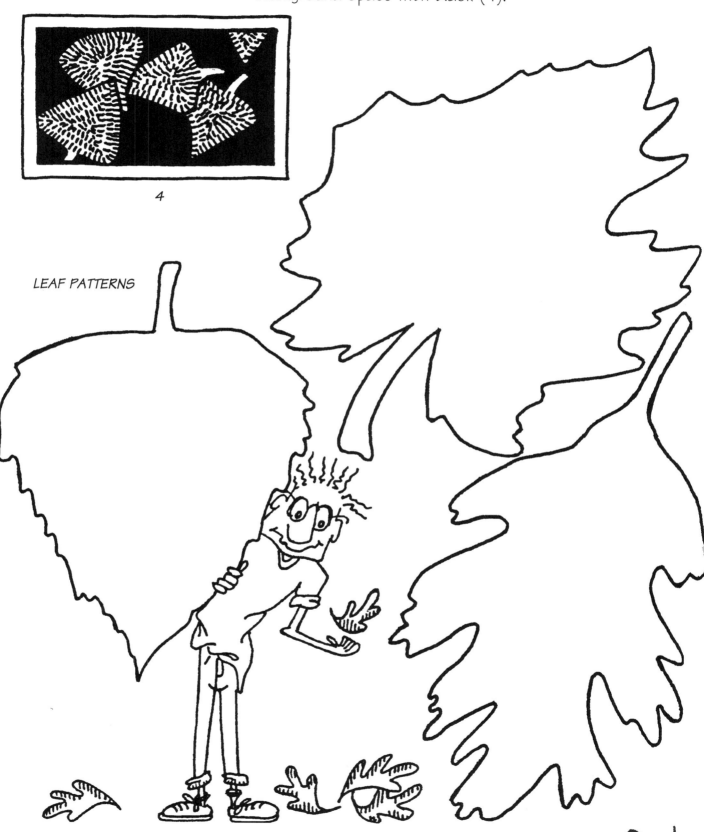

4

LEAF PATTERNS

From *Adventures with Art*, published by GoodYearBooks. Copyright © 1993 Sarah Jenkins and Margaret Foote.

As the leaves drift gently to the ground.

Tempera Trees

Materials

Each Child Needs:
- ○ 9" x 12" piece of manila art paper
- ○ plastic straws
- ○ pencil
- ○ crayons
- ○ black tempera paint (thinned)
- ○ container for paint
- ○ spoon
- ○ newspaper

Easy

CONCEPTS

Shape Design

Directions

Have the children:

1. Place a spoonful of black tempera at the bottom of the art paper (1).

2. Using the straw, blow the paint upward on the paper. This will form the trunk and branches of a tree. (To form smaller limbs, use the straw as a brush.) (2)

3. After the tree has dried, use crayons to make a picture (3). Make sure the tree is thoroughly dry before using the crayons.

4. Add paint to areas that need to be filled in.

1

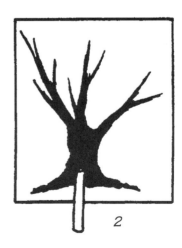

2

From Adventures with Art, published by GoodYearBooks. Copyright © 1993 Sarah Jenkins and Margaret Foote.

To lose yourself in your art is really okay,

Suggestions

1. Children can do three or five overlapping trees in bright colors to create an underwater ocean scene (4). Make sure each tree is dry before a child goes on to the next one. Have them cut out ocean creatures and glue them on the picture.

2. Have the children make watercolor landscapes. When they are done with the landscapes, they can add a tempera tree to each (5).

3

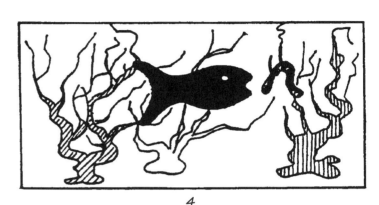

4

5

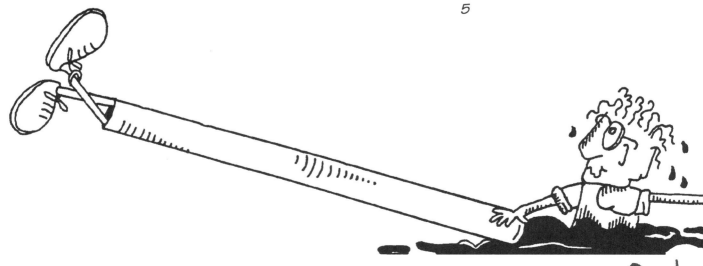

But, you know we didn't mean it this way.

Texture Turkeys

Materials

Each Child Needs:
- pencil
- crayons
- turkey pattern (enlarge page 35 on a copy machine or have students draw their own pattern)
- 12" x 18" piece of colored construction paper
- 9" x 12" or 12" x 18" piece of white drawing paper
- scissors

Easy

CONCEPTS

Texture Line

Directions

Before getting started, discuss texture with the children. Show examples on the board. Give each child a turkey pattern.

Then, have the children:

1. Trace the turkey pattern on the white paper, drawing in wings and a wattle (1).

2. Fill in textures on the turkey, using no less then 8 different textures. Use a variety of colors, too (2).

3. Cut out the turkey and glue it on the colored paper. Cut the colored paper around the turkey so that a border of approximately 1 inch remains. Display it with others in the classroom.

1

2

It's turkey time, and Art is out for the hunt,

From *Adventures with Art*, published by GoodYearBooks. Copyright © 1993 Sarah Jenkins and Margaret Foote.

Suggestions

1. Unusual textures and colors can be used for dramatic effect. Use the techniques discussed on page 14 to create a variety of textures.

2. For a neater look, use smaller textures (textures with smaller patterns).

3. You can make different textures with rubbings by placing paper over objects and rubbing on the paper with a crayon.

TURKEY PATTERN

Who's catching whom, if we might be so blunt?

Sandscapes

Materials

Each Child Needs:
- ○ 8-1/2" x 5-1/2" piece of sandpaper
- ○ crayons
- ○ 8-1/2" x 5-1/2" piece of white drawing paper
- ○ 9" x 6" piece of black construction paper
- ○ newspaper

Also Needed:
- ○ an iron

Easy

CONCEPTS

Texture Design

Directions

Before getting started, discuss with children objects found in a landscape (mountains, sky, trees, etc.). Then discuss with them the concepts "horizon line," "background," and "foreground." (For a brush-up, see page 11.) Hand out the sandpaper.

Then, have the children:

1. Draw a simple landscape on the sandpaper. Color the landscape darkly (1).

2. Have an adult place newspaper under the colored sandpaper and iron the sandpaper onto a piece of drawing paper, design side down (2).

3. Peel the sandpaper off of the drawing paper. Glue the picture onto a larger piece of black paper, giving the picture a border (3).

Art thought of this project on a whim,

From *Adventures with Art*, published by GoodYearBooks. Copyright © 1993 Sarah Jenkins and Margaret Foote.

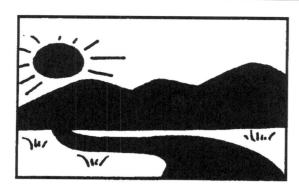

1

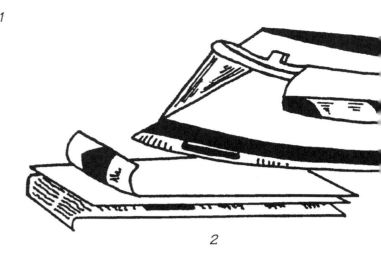

2

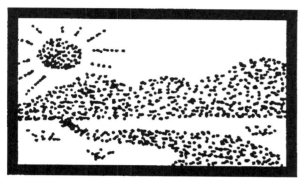

3

Suggestions

1. This is a great project for a unit on Native American art. Discuss Native American symbols and then have the children draw the symbols directly onto the sandpaper. Do not iron the sandpaper. Have children cut the sandpaper pictures in the shape of rugs (4).

2. Have the children draw a mountain on a piece of cardboard and then divide the mountain into rock layers. Mix glue with different colors of tempera paint, and have the children place a different color of glue in each section of the mountain. Then have them sprinkle regular table salt onto the glue in each section (5). The salt gives the picture a look of sand. You can also mix dry tempera paint with salt or sand and then glue in the different sections.

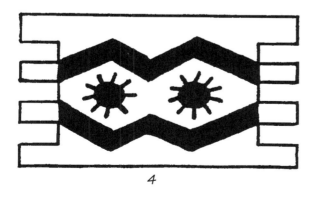

4

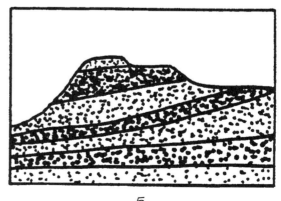

5

And it did make quite an impression on him.

Paper Punch Trees

Materials

Each Child Needs:
- ○ 9" x 12" piece of manila paper
- ○ colored chalk
- ○ glue
- ○ pencil
- ○ paper punch
- ○ fixative
- ○ large quantity of construction-paper punched holes in various colors (dark green, orange, yellow, red)

Intermediate

CONCEPTS

Balance Shape

Directions

Before getting started, discuss with the children the blending and shading of a tree trunk and its limbs, including using browns, blacks, and highlights. Give each child a piece of manila paper.

Then, have the children:

1. Use the pencil to sketch a tree trunk and tree branches (1).

2. Blend and shade the tree and the background (2).

3. Ask an adult to spray fixative on the picture to prevent smearing.

4. Arrange and glue paper punch holes on the limbs and ground in the picture (3).

Suggestions

1. Have the children punch the holes ahead of time. (This project requires a lot of punched holes.)

2. Use different shades of green paper to make this either a spring or a summer picture. Shades of yellow, red, and orange create a Fall effect.

From *Adventures with Art*, published by GoodYearBooks. Copyright © 1993 Sarah Jenkins and Margaret Foote.

Out on a limb, Art trembles with fear,

1

2

3

Is there a slight resemblance here?

Native American Portraits

Materials

Advanced

CONCEPTS

Balance Shading

Each Child Needs:

○ 12" x 18" piece of white drawing paper
○ pencil
○ crayons
○ charts (eyes, noses, mouths—see the examples below; you can draw these up ahead of time for the children)
○ pictures of Native Americans (be sure to select pictures that are not stereo-typical but instead are indicative of actual Native American life)

Directions

Before getting started, display the photos of Native Americans in the room. Discuss with the children how to draw head and facial features proportionately. Discuss different shapes of heads:

ROUND

OVAL

SQUARE

Discuss placement of facial features:

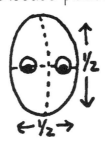

EYES

NOSE

MOUTH

Then, have the children:

1. Use a pencil to draw the head and shoulders of their Native American.

2. Select features from the charts of eyes, noses, and mouths. Complete the picture (1).

3. Color the picture, shading in the appropriate areas (nose, eyes, cheeks, chin, feathers, etc.).

40

FALL

Art traveled west with the setting sun,

From Adventures with Art, published by GoodYearBooks. Copyright © 1993 Sarah Jenkins and Margaret Foote.

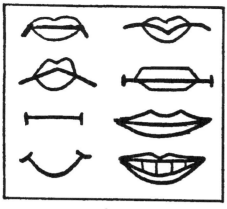

MOUTHS

EYES AND EYEBROWS

1

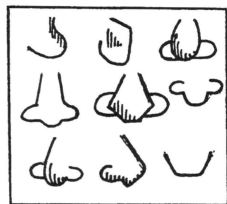

NOSES

Suggestions

1. This project is best done in two days.

2. This could be a self-portrait or used to represent people of other lands or time periods.

Now he's at rest, for the day is done.

Disguise Turkeys

Materials

Each Child Needs:
- ○ 9" x 12" piece of white drawing paper
- ○ pencil
- ○ crayons

Intermediate

CONCEPTS

Shape Design

Directions

Before getting started, discuss the idea of using a disguise. Why would a turkey want a disguise at Thanksgiving time?

Discuss basic turkey shapes (1). Display the turkey pattern from page 35, or draw one of your own and display it in the classroom (2).

Then, have the children:

1. Select an unusual disguise for a turkey.

2. Draw a turkey shape. Finish the picture by adding a costume or disguise.

1

Be careful who you meet on the wild frontier,

From *Adventures with Art*, published by GoodYearBooks. Copyright © 1993 Sarah Jenkins and Margaret Foote.

-HUNTER-

2

For things are not always as they appear.

Winter

Time moves on,
    the season turns,
There are many more concepts
    to be learned.
With paint and glitter, chalk and more,
A variety of projects are in store.

Winter winds on a snowy day,
the faraway sounds of bells on a sleigh.
        The journey continues,
            Art's on a roll.
        Be careful Art,
            watch out for that hole!

Carolers

Materials

Each Child Needs:
- ⭘ 9" x 12" piece of oaktag or stiff white paper
- ⭘ 4" x 7" piece of art paper
- ⭘ crayons
- ⭘ scissors
- ⭘ pencil
- ⭘ cottonball
- ⭘ glue

Intermediate

CONCEPTS

Shape Balance

Directions

Have the children:

1. Fold the oaktag into thirds (1).

2. Draw the outline of a person on one third of the oaktag. Add a scarf and hat. Make the feet flat and draw the arms so that they extend off the paper (2).

3. Cut on the outline, but cut through all three layers of oaktag.

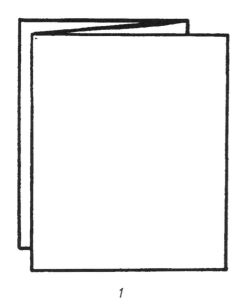

1

2

From *Adventures with Art*, published by GoodYearBooks. Copyright © 1993 Sarah Jenkins and Margaret Foote.

Art lifts his head as he begins to croon,

4. Draw facial features and details on hats and scarves. Draw the eyes and mouths large and open. Color each caroler with a different set of analogous colors. Glue cotton to the tops of the hats for tassels (3)

3

5. Fold the 4" x 7" piece of paper in half and then unfold the paper (4). About 1/2" up on each free arm, make a fold (5). Glue the paper to the folded sections of the free arms. Let dry.

6. Stand the carolers on their feet (6).

4

5

6

From *Adventures with Art*, published by GoodYearBooks. Copyright © 1993 Sarah Jenkins and Margaret Foote.

Too bad he can't carry a tune.

Glittering Bells

Materials

Each Child Needs:
- ○ 9" x 12" piece of black construction paper
- ○ tissue paper
- ○ glitter
- ○ glue
- ○ scissors
- ○ pencil

Directions

Have the children:

1. Fold the black paper in half (1).

2. Draw half of a bell on one side of the folded paper (2).

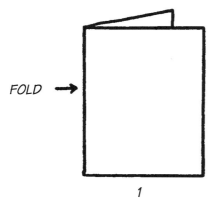

FOLD →

1

2

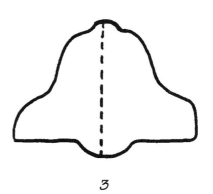

3

3. With the black paper folded, cut out the bell. Cut out sections, cutting in from the fold and cutting through both layers of paper (3 and 4).

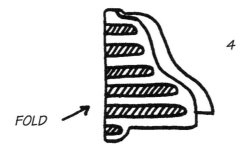

4

FOLD ↗

From *Adventures with Art*, published by GoodYearBooks. Copyright © 1993 Sarah Jenkins and Margaret Foote.

The sound of bells rings loud and clear,

4. Select a color of tissue paper and glue it to the back of the bell. Trim off the excess tissue.

5. Glue glitter on the front of the bell (5). Then display the bells in the classroom.

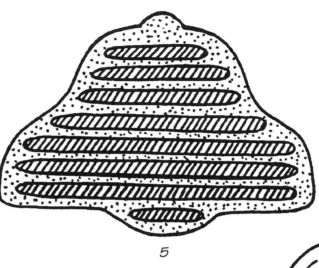

5

Suggestions

1. Have the children fold the paper more than once so that the bells come out in a strand, like paper dolls (6).

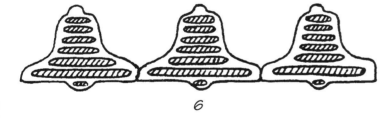

6

2. When you hang one bell, it will spin around and you won't always be able to see the decorated front. Instead, cut out two bells and hang them together, back to back (7).

7

Unfortunately, it's much too near.

Bethlehem Star

Materials

Each Child Needs:
- 9" x 12" piece of white drawing paper
- 4-1/4" x 17" piece of black construction paper
- pencil
- crayons
- glitter
- scissors
- glue

Intermediate

CONCEPTS

Color Design

Directions

Have the children:

1. Draw a star at the top center of the white paper (1).

2. Choose four analogous colors. Using the lightest color, draw vertical strokes around the star. Color darkly (2).

3. Repeat the stroke, going from lightest to darkest until the whole page is covered (3). Make sure no white paper shows through the strokes.

From *Adventures with Art*, published by GoodYearBooks. Copyright © 1993 Sarah Jenkins and Margaret Foote.

Atop a hill, Art watches in awe,

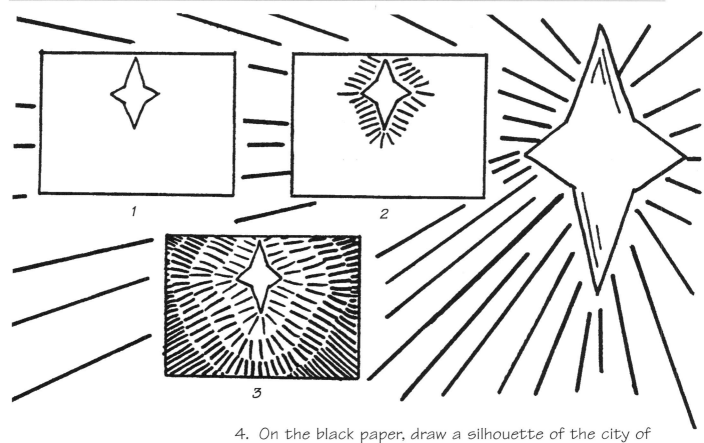

4. On the black paper, draw a silhouette of the city of Bethlehem (4).

5. Glue the silhouette to the bottom of the white paper. Fill in the star with glitter. Make 5 or 6 rays going out from the star with glitter (5). Let dry.

6. Display the stars in the classroom.

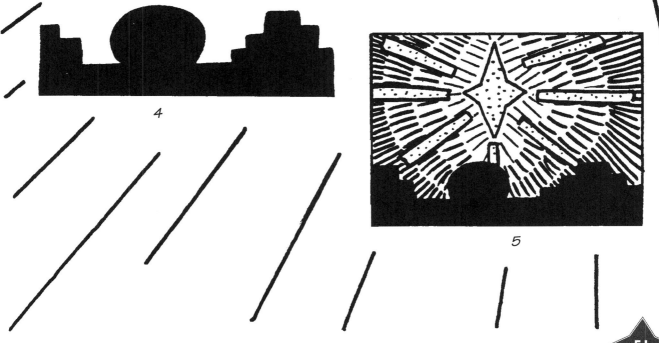

One brilliant stare was all he saw.

Mirrored Menorahs

Materials

Intermediate

CONCEPTS

Line Balance (symmetry)

Each Child Needs:
- ○ 9" x 12" piece of white drawing paper
- ○ pencil
- ○ menorah pattern, enlarged on a copying machine
- ○ glue
- ○ colored pencils

Directions

Before getting started, display pictures of menorahs. Talk about what they are and how they are used during Hanukkah.

Then, have the children:

1. Glue the menorah pattern to one half of the 9" x 12" piece of white paper (1).

2. Using a pencil, draw the other half of the menorah. Remember, both sides should match (2).

3. Using the colored pencils, color the entire menorah. Keep in mind the rules of shading (3).

1

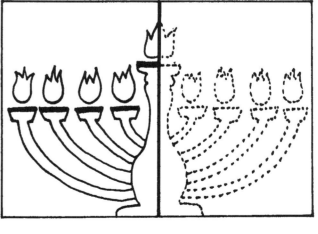

2

From *Adventures with Art*, published by GoodYearBooks. Copyright © 1993 Sarah Jenkins and Margaret Foote.

Art's job it is to light nine lights,

Suggestions

Make your own pattern. Then have a friend finish it.

3

PATTERN

From *Adventures with Art*, published by GoodYearBooks. Copyright © 1993 Sarah Jenkins and Margaret Foote.

So the menorah may burn through the holiday bright.

Wandering Wisemen

Materials

Each Child Needs:

○ wiseman and camel patterns, enlarged on a copying machine
○ 9" x 12" piece of brown construction paper
○ foil holiday gift wrap
○ pencil
○ scissors
○ black crayon
○ glue
○ 6" length of string

Intermediate

CONCEPTS

**Shape
Texture
Design**

Directions

Have the children:

1. Outline the camel in black on the brown paper and cut it out.

2. Cut out the wiseman.

3. Place the wiseman on the printed side of the foil (1). Trace around the wiseman with a pencil, and cut him out (2).

4. From the foil cut-out, cut the wiseman's face and his hand. This gives you his robe and hat (3).

1

2

3

Riding a camel is not Art's forté,

From *Adventures with Art*, published by GoodYearBooks. Copyright © 1993 Sarah Jenkins and Margaret Foote.

5. Glue the hat and robe on the brown paper. Using a black crayon, color in the facial features (4).

6. Glue the wiseman on the camel. Glue string from the camel's head to the wiseman's hand (5).

4

5

CAMEL PATTERN (ENLARGE)

WISEMAN PATTERN (ENLARGE)

Is he really trying, or is this just horseplay?

Spongy Snowpeople

Materials

Each Child Needs:
- ○ 9" x 12" piece of blue construction paper
- ○ white tempera paint
- ○ crayons
- ○ sponge, 1" x 1"
- ○ pencil

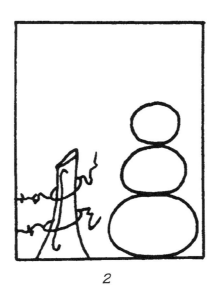

Easy

CONCEPTS

Texture
Balance

Directions

Have the children:

1. Using a pencil, draw a fencepost surrounded with wires on one side of the paper (1).

2. Next to the fencepost, draw three circles, each smaller than the one below, for a snowperson (2).

3. Dip the sponge into the paint. Gently dab the sponge on the ground, post, and snowperson, giving the effect of snow (3).

4. Add details to the snowperson with crayons (4).

From *Adventures with Art*, published by GoodYearBooks. Copyright © 1993 Sarah Jenkins and Margaret Foote.

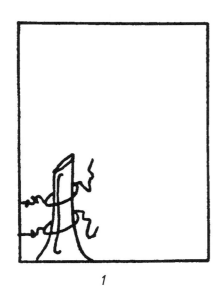

1

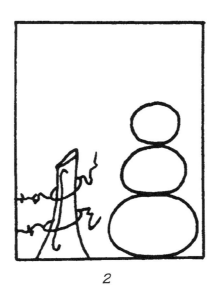

2

3

Hold on Art, don't be sucked in,

4

Suggestions

1. Use a sponge to create flowers, cattails, and trees in a picture (5).

2. Using a "natural" sponge will give a unique effect. You will find this type of sponge at a beauty supply store.

5

You're our hero, we know you can win.

Stained Glass Windows

Materials

Intermediate

CONCEPTS

**Design
Texture**

Each Child Needs:
- ○ 9" x 12" piece of white drawing paper
- ○ 9" x 12" piece of black construction paper
- ○ food coloring (several different colors)
- ○ liquid dish soap
- ○ various containers (milk cartons, plastic bottles, etc.)
- ○ newspaper
- ○ pencil
- ○ scissors
- ○ water
- ○ straw

Directions

Before getting started, set up a work area with newspaper on the table and floor. In the various containers, mix the water with 3 or 4 drops of dish soap and food colorings to attain the desired colors.

Give each child a piece of white paper and a piece of black paper.

Then, have the children:

1. Using a straw, blow bubbles in the paint mixture (1). Place the white paper directly on the bubbles (2). Repeat the process with all of the different paints until the entire paper is covered with different-colored bubble prints (3). Let dry.

1

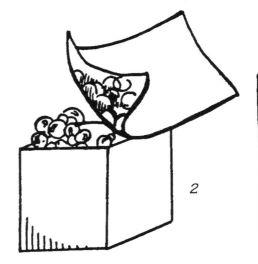
2

3

We must save Art, he's in serious trouble,

From *Adventures with Art*, published by GoodYearBooks. Copyright © 1993 Sarah Jenkins and Margaret Foote.

2. Fold the black paper in half. Draw half of a church window with a pencil on one half of the paper. Round off the corners at the top (4).

3. Cut out the window sections. Be sure to cut through both layers of the folded paper (5).

4. Place the window frame on top of the bubble art. Glue the two pieces together. Trim the edges around the window frame (6).

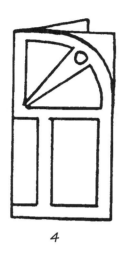

4

5

6

Suggestions

Use the bubble paper for stationery or wrapping paper.

But do we really want to burst his bubble?

Slices of Winter

Materials

Each Child Needs:
- 9" x 12" piece of white construction paper
- 6" x 9" piece of blue construction paper
- scraps of black, orange, brown, red, and white construction paper
- pencil
- scissors
- glue

Intermediate

CONCEPTS

Balance
Shape

Directions

Have the children:

1. Draw one small, one medium, and one large circle on the blue paper. Use the entire piece of paper.

2. Cut the large circle into 1/2" strips. Glue the strips on the large white paper, leaving a space between each one. (Hint: The uncut circles should only fill half of the white paper.) (1)

3. Do the same with the small and medium circles.

4. Use the colored-paper scraps to add a hat, arms, mittens, carrot nose, eyes, and scarf (2).

1

From *Adventures with Art*, published by GoodYearBooks. Copyright © 1993 Sarah Jenkins and Margaret Foote.

Piece by piece, the snowman grows,

Suggestions

Animals and other shapes are also excellent for this activity (3).

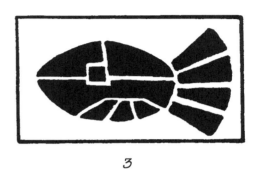

2

3

Art, are you sure that's the right pose?

Striking Snowflakes

Materials

Each Child Needs:
- ○ two 9" x 9" pieces of white construction paper
- ○ one 9" x 9" piece of black construction paper
- ○ 9" x 1" strips of tissue paper, three strips of each of three colors
- ○ glue
- ○ scissors

Intermediate

CONCEPTS

Balance
Design
Color (contrast)

Directions

Have the children:

1. Glue the tissue strips on one of the pieces of white paper. Use only 3 or 4 drops of glue on each strip. Glue them in the following pattern (1):

| LIGHT BLUE | VIOLET | PINK | LIGHT BLUE | VIOLET | PINK | LIGHT BLUE | VIOLET | PINK |

1

2. Fold the other white square four times and cut out a snowflake pattern. Use the whole paper for the snowflake (2).

From *Adventures with Art*, published by GoodYearBooks. Copyright © 1993 Sarah Jenkins and Margaret Foote.

Snowflakes fall, no two the same,

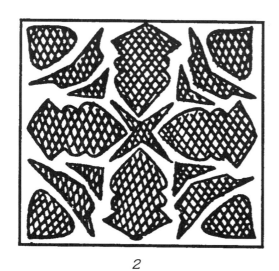

2

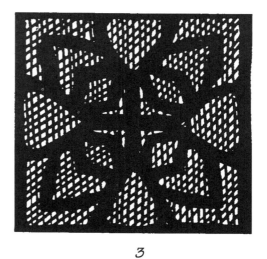

3

3. Do the same with the black square (3). Make a different pattern on the black paper than on the white paper.

4. Glue the white snowflake on top of the tissue paper. Then glue on the black snowflake (4).

4

Then, out of nowhere, down it came!

Outfold Objects

Materials

Each Child Needs:
- ○ 12" x 12" piece of white drawing paper
- ○ 6" x 6" piece of colored construction paper
- ○ pencil
- ○ scissors
- ○ glue

Intermediate

CONCEPTS

Balance Shape

Directions

Have the children:

1. Draw abstract shapes on the colored paper with a pencil. Make sure each shape is connected to the edge of the paper but none of the shapes overlap (1).

2. Cut out the shapes. Arrange the square, with shapes cut out, on the white paper. Place the shapes outside the box, on the white paper, so that they meet the place where you cut them from the square. (The cut-out shapes will be used to give the effect of negative space.)

   Make sure the square and shapes touch (2).

3. After allowing enough space for the shapes, glue them and the square to the white paper.

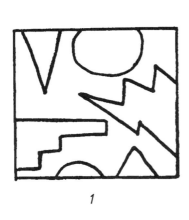

1

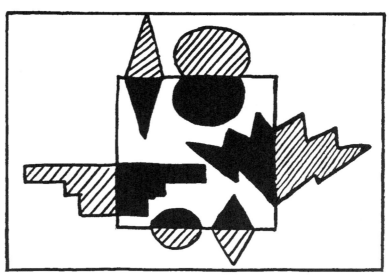

2

From Adventures with Art, published by GoodYearBooks. Copyright © 1993 Sarah Jenkins and Margaret Foote.

Bend him, fold him, tie him with string,

Suggestions

1. By cutting mountains, clouds, or other realistic shapes from the original square, children can create specific scenes (3).

2. Of course, they can also use abstract shapes of their choice to create the design.

3. Have children experiment with circles or other geometric shapes (4).

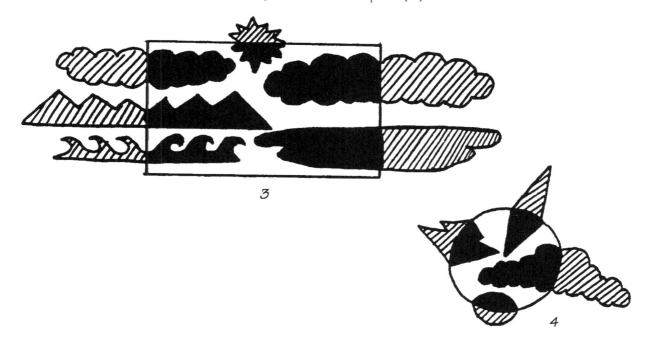

3

4

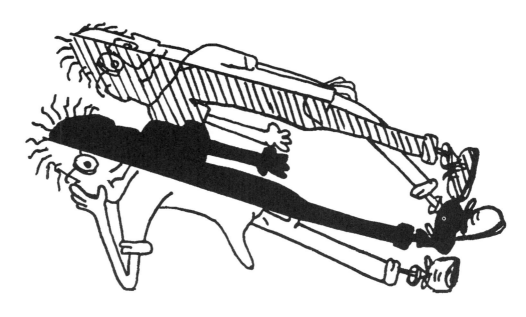

Our flexible Art can do anything.

Famous Faces

Materials

Each Child Needs:
- ○ 8" x 17" piece of white construction paper
- ○ 9" x 12" piece of black construction paper
- ○ pencil
- ○ scissors
- ○ pictures of statesmen and stateswomen

Advanced

CONCEPTS

Line Design

Directions

Before getting started, display the pictures of prominent American statespeople in the classroom. Discuss with the children any prominent facial features in these pictures. Hand out the white paper.

Then, have the children:

1. Draw the features and facial lines of a statesperson (1).

2. Separate each line by forming it into a block section (2). Give the lines thickness, and then separate them into sections.

1

2

Is that you, Art, standing tall?

From *Adventures with Art*, published by GoodYearBooks. Copyright © 1993 Sarah Jenkins and Margaret Foote.

3. Cut out each section carefully. You will need to poke the scissors into the sections, rather than cutting into the paper from the edges.

4. Center the white paper on the black paper. Glue the two pieces together (3).

3

Suggestions

1. Try this activity with black paper on a white background (4).

2. Try this activity with objects instead of people (5).

4

5

1

Be careful now, or you might fall.

Hanging Hearts

From *Adventures with Art*, published by GoodYearBooks. Copyright © 1993 Sarah Jenkins and Margaret Foote.

Materials

Each Child Needs:
- ◯ three 2" x 6" pink construction paper strips
- ◯ two 2" x 9" red construction paper strips
- ◯ two 2" x 12" pink construction paper strips
- ◯ two 2" x 18" red construction paper strips

Also Needed:
- ◯ stapler

Easy

CONCEPTS

Balance Shape

Directions

Have the children:

1. Begin with one 2" x 6" pink strip. On each side of this strip, place the other strips in this order (1):

   1st   2" x 18" red

   2nd   2" x 12" pink

   3rd   2" x 9" red

   4th   2" x 6" pink

2. Make all strips even at the top. Ask an adult to staple the pile of strips twice at the top (2).

2

 With bow and arrow, Art starts out,

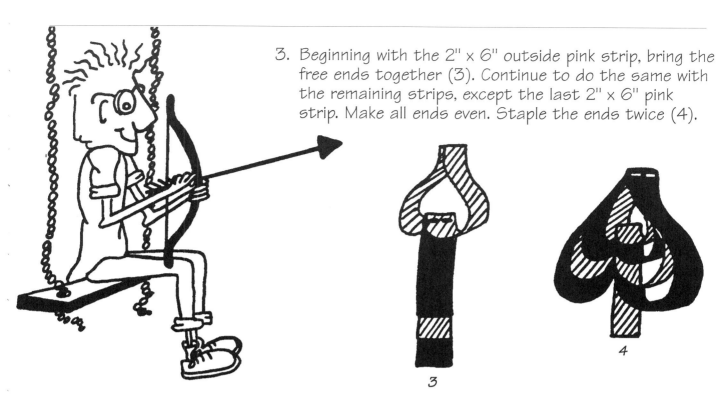

3. Beginning with the 2" x 6" outside pink strip, bring the free ends together (3). Continue to do the same with the remaining strips, except the last 2" x 6" pink strip. Make all ends even. Staple the ends twice (4).

3

4

4. Turn the art upside down. Punch a hole in the 2" x 6" pink strip in the middle and hang the heart in the classroom using a straightened paper clip (5).

5

Assisting Cupid on his route.

Overlapping Hearts

Materials

Each Child Needs:
- ⭘ 9" x 12" piece of white construction paper
- ⭘ pencil
- ⭘ crayons
- ⭘ heart patterns
- ⭘ thin black marker

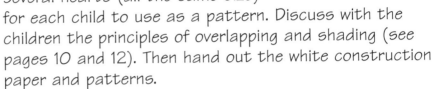

Easy

CONCEPTS

Perspective (overlapping) Shape

Directions

Before getting started, cut out several hearts (all the same size) for each child to use as a pattern. Discuss with the children the principles of overlapping and shading (see pages 10 and 12). Then hand out the white construction paper and patterns.

Then, have the children:

1. Using a pencil, draw the heart pattern randomly on the paper. Where hearts overlap, erase the extra lines. Draw some hearts going off the page to make the design even more interesting (1).

2. Using three colors, shade the hearts from darker on the edges to lighter in the center (2).

3. Outline all of the hearts with a black marker.

1

A shower of arrows from up above,

From *Adventures with Art*, published by GoodYearBooks. Copyright © 1993 Sarah Jenkins and Margaret Foote.

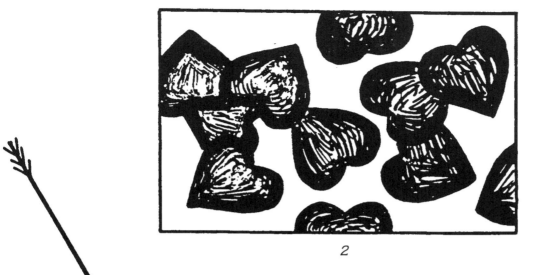

2

Suggestions

1. Use an odd number of heart shapes in the picture.

2. Try this activity with a different shape, especially at other holidays.

It's hit and miss, this game of love!

Spring

Days get warmer, blossoms appear,
Nature is telling us that spring is here.
Bubbles, seeds, and tissue, too,
Many more plans for you to do.

A gentle breeze on a bright blue day
Can quickly lift your cares away.
Art takes time for a little repose,
Then the trek continues and off he goes!

Pencil Particulars

Materials

Each Child Needs:
- ○ 2" x 18" piece of white drawing paper
- ○ 2 pencils
- ○ ruler
- ○ 19" x 13" piece of black paper

Intermediate

CONCEPTS

Line

Directions

Do this project ahead of time so you have a sample to show the class. While they look at the sample, discuss shading. Make sure the children are aware of the source of light in the picture and how the source affects the placement of shadows. Hand out the drawing paper and pencils.

Then, have the children:

1. Use one of the pencils as a model. Look carefully at the pencil, observing the lines, detail, and shadows.

2. Draw the basic lines of the pencil (1). Use a ruler as a straightedge if needed. Draw the pencil as long as the paper.

3. Shade the pencil. Make sure to draw in the pencil's shadow. The darkest sections of the drawing are the pencil lead and the section of pencil's shadow that is closest to the pencil. Pay attention to how the light reflects on the pencil (2).

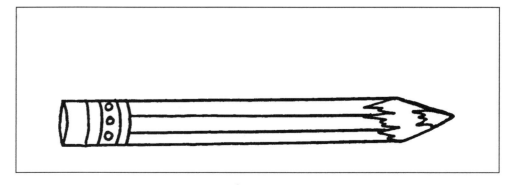

1

From *Adventures with Art*, published by GoodYearBooks. Copyright © 1993 Sarah Jenkins and Margaret Foote.

Maybe if Art had been to the gym,

4. Center the finished drawing on black paper. Glue.

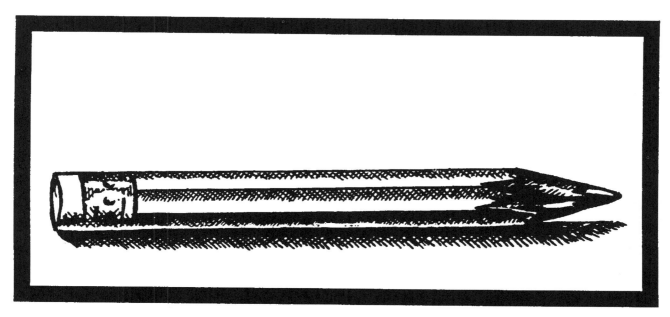

2

This exercise would be easy for him.

Multicolor Leprechauns

Materials

Each Child Needs:

○ 9" x 2" strip of each of the following colors of construction paper:

- purple
- red
- orange
- green
- yellow
- blue

○ 9" x 12" piece of pink construction paper
○ 9" x 12" piece of white construction paper
○ 4" x 6" piece of black construction paper
○ 3" x 4" piece of white construction paper
○ scissors
○ crayons
○ 2 cotton balls
○ glue

Directions

Have the children:

1. Glue the 9" x 2" strips of paper on the 9" x 12" piece of white paper. Use this order for the strips:

RED
ORANGE
YELLOW
GREEN
BLUE
PURPLE

In order to win this game of luck,

From *Adventures with Art*, published by GoodYearBooks. Copyright © 1993 Sarah Jenkins and Margaret Foote.

2. On the 9" x 12" piece of pink paper, draw a leprechaun face. Make the ears large (1). Cut large eyes out of the 3" x 4" piece of white paper and the 4" x 6" piece of black paper (2). Cut out little white pieces for the pupil of each eye (3). Glue the eye pieces to the leprechaun's face.

3. Color in the rest of the facial features, except the hair and beard (4). Cut out the entire face. Tear the cottonballs apart and glue the cotton on the face where the hair and beard should be.

4. Glue the entire face to the rainbow background from step 1. Cut a hat out of black paper and glue this on the leprechaun's head (5).

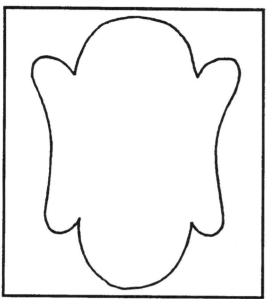

1

2

3

4

5

Suggestions

1. Try making a rainbow background using watercolors instead of paper.

2. For a different look, add a bow tie to the leprechaun.

Art needs to show a little pluck.

Spring Silhouettes

Materials

Each Child Needs:
- ○ 9" x 12" piece of white construction paper
- ○ 9" x 12" piece of black construction paper
- ○ pencil
- ○ scissors
- ○ white crayon
- ○ glue

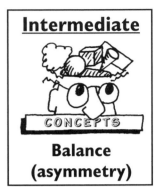

Intermediate

CONCEPTS

Balance (asymmetry)

Directions

Have the children:

1. Choose a spring object, like a butterfly, flower, or bird. Draw one large and two small silhouettes of that object on white paper. Cut out the silhouettes (1).

1

2. On the black paper, use a white crayon to draw a border one inch from the edge on all sides.

3. Glue the silhouettes on the black paper inside the border (2).

It's obvious Art loves this time of year,

From Adventures with Art, published by GoodYearBooks. Copyright © 1993 Sarah Jenkins and Margaret Foote.

2

Suggestions

You can reverse the look of the finished piece by cutting the silhouettes from black paper and gluing them on white paper. Use a black marker to make the border on the white paper.

Do you think he's aware that others are near?

Seed Mosaics

Materials

Each Child Needs:
○ assorted seeds, beans, macaroni and cereal (brought by children)
○ 8" x 8" cardboard square
○ glue
○ pencil
○ example of a mosaic

Easy

CONCEPTS

Texture Design

Directions

Before getting started, discuss mosaics with the children. Show them the sample. Hand out the cardboard squares.

Then, have the children:

1. Select an item from one of these categories:
   • animals (fish, butterflies, birds, etc.)
   • plants (flowers, vegetables, trees, etc.)
   • miscellaneous (buildings, food, vehicles, etc.)

2. Decide which seeds are best for the picture. Different seeds and beans have different textures, which create different effects in a mosaic.

3. Draw the outline of the chosen item with a pencil on cardboard (1). Make the object as large as the cardboard.

1

From *Adventures with Art*, published by GoodYearBooks. Copyright © 1993 Sarah Jenkins and Margaret Foote.

 Art has fun being a scarecrow,

4. Glue one seed or bean at a time to the picture, putting the glue on the cardboard, not the seed (2).

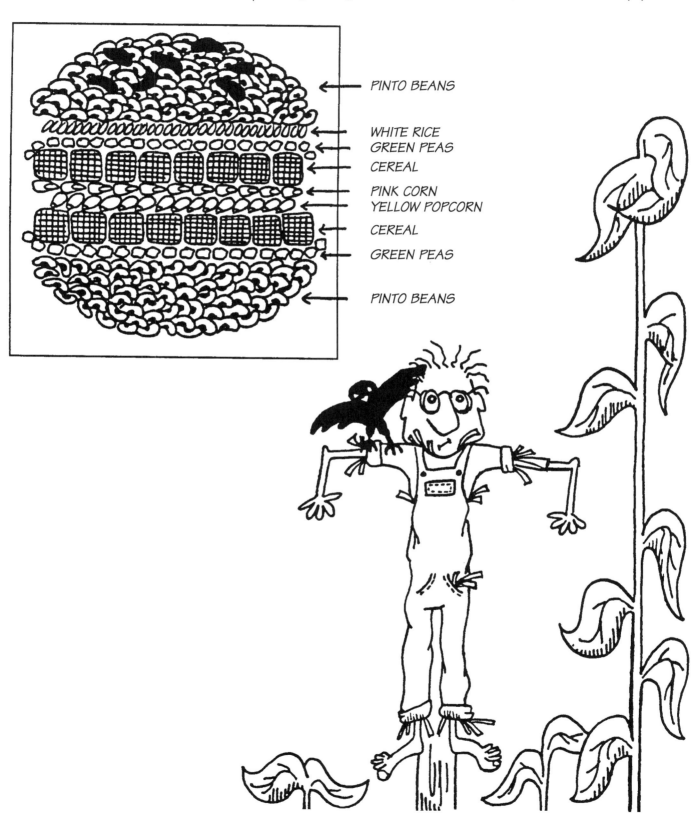

PINTO BEANS

WHITE RICE
GREEN PEAS
CEREAL

PINK CORN
YELLOW POPCORN
CEREAL

GREEN PEAS

PINTO BEANS

Just hangin' around watchin' seeds grow.

Foil Wraparounds

Materials

Each Child Needs:
- ○ 9" x 12" piece of oaktag
- ○ 10" x 13" sheet of tin foil
- ○ yarn (any color)
- ○ markers
- ○ pencils
- ○ scissors
- ○ glue

Intermediate

CONCEPTS

**Line
Texture**

Directions

Have the children:

1. Choose a simple object. Draw the object on the oaktag, using most of the paper (1).

2. Glue the yarn on the lines of the picture (2).

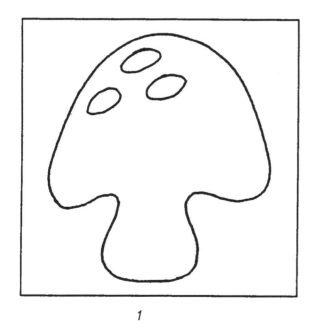

1

2

3. Place the tin foil squarely on top of the oaktag. Fold the foil tightly around the edges of the paper.

Art makes an impression wherever he's been,

From *Adventures with Art*, published by GoodYearBooks. Copyright © 1993 Sarah Jenkins and Margaret Foote.

4. Press the foil firmly around the yarn shape, being careful not to rip the foil (3).

5. Using markers, color in the indented spaces. This will define the object (4).

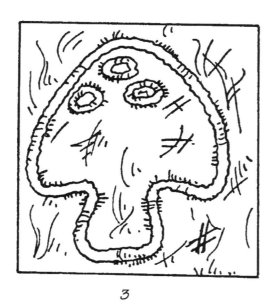
3

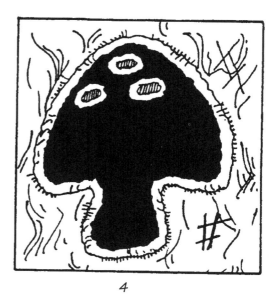
4

Suggestions

You can also make tin foil pictures of scenes, not just objects. To do so, draw an object. Then cut out the object and the section of the picture below it. This will add a skyline. Continue with the project using steps 3 to 5 above (5).

5

What happened, Art, foiled again?

Clowning Around

Materials

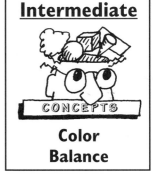

Intermediate

CONCEPTS

Color Balance

Each Child Needs:

○ two 12" x 16" sheets of tissue paper, each a different color

○ two 8" x 6" sheets of tissue paper, each a different color

○ 4" x 12" piece of white construction paper

○ 9" x 12" piece of pink construction paper

○ 9" x 12" piece of white construction paper

○ 9" x 12" piece of blue construction paper

○ pencil

○ crayons

○ scissors

○ pictures of clowns

Also Needed:

○ stapler

Directions

Before getting started, display the pictures of clowns in the room. Discuss with the children how to draw head and facial features proportionately. Discuss different shapes of heads:

ROUND

OVAL

SQUARE

Discuss placement of facial features:

EYES

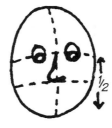

NOSE

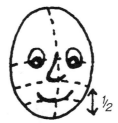

MOUTH

Then, have the children:

1. Fold the pink paper (either way, depending on the shape of face desired). Draw half of the head shape, including hair, on the paper (1). Cut out the head, making sure to cut through both layers of folded paper (2).

Clowning around is easy to do,

From *Adventures with Art*, published by GoodYearBooks. Copyright © 1993 Sarah Jenkins and Margaret Foote.

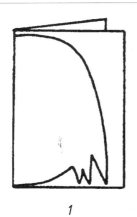

1

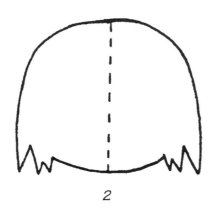

2

3

2. Draw the features, using the placement discussed earlier. Add clown make-up around the eyes, mouth, nose, and cheeks. Color the face (3).

3. Cut a collar or bow tie out of white paper. Cut a round ball out of white paper. This will be the pompom on the top of the hat.

4. Cut a hat, hands, and feet from blue paper.

5. Gather both ends of all tissue pieces. Staple twice at each end (4).

6. Assemble the clown according to this guide (5):

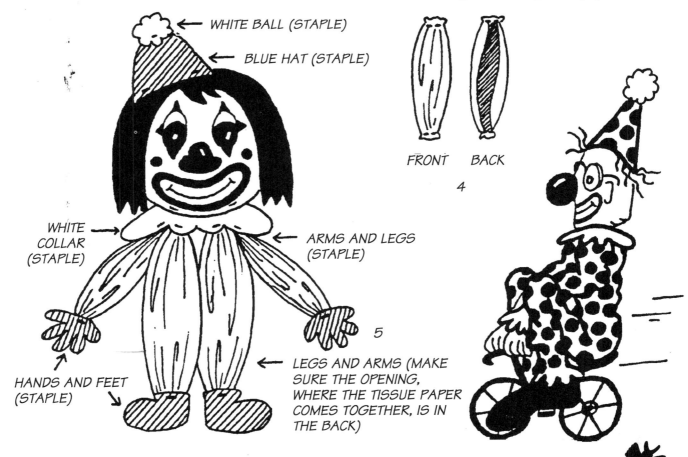

WHITE BALL (STAPLE)

BLUE HAT (STAPLE)

WHITE COLLAR (STAPLE)

ARMS AND LEGS (STAPLE)

HANDS AND FEET (STAPLE)

LEGS AND ARMS (MAKE SURE THE OPENING, WHERE THE TISSUE PAPER COMES TOGETHER, IS IN THE BACK)

FRONT   BACK

4

5

Except when the bike is too little for you.

Soft Chalk

Materials

Each Child Needs:
- ○ colored chalk
- ○ two 12" x 12" pieces of white drawing paper
- ○ facial tissues
- ○ scissors
- ○ pencil
- ○ newspaper

Also Needed:
- ○ fixative

Intermediate

CONCEPTS

**Texture
Color**

Directions

Before getting started, cover the work area with newspaper, and hand out the white paper.

Then, have the children:

1. Fold one of the white art squares into a triangle (1). Fold it in half again, creating another triangle (2).

2. On the edge where there is not a fold, draw a design 1/2" from the edge (3). Cut out the design, making sure to cut through all layers of the folded paper (4).

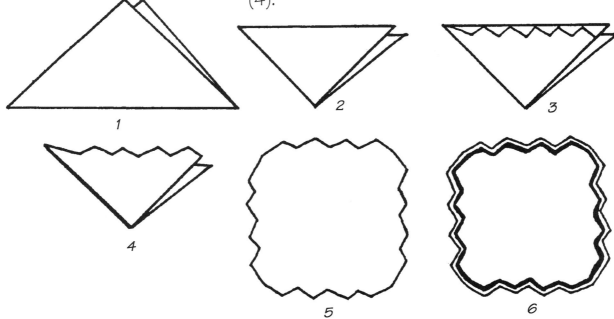

1

2

3

4

5

6

From Adventures with Art, published by GoodYearBooks. Copyright © 1993 Sarah Jenkins and Margaret Foote.

When Art sneezes, it won't be slight,

3. Unfold the paper (5). Put a line of chalk around the edge of the paper. Press firmly so that the line is thick and dark (6). Also, remember that the darkest colors go on the outside edge of the picture while the lightest colors go inside.

4. Center the square with the design on top of the other sheet of paper.

5. Hold the design down with one hand. With the other hand, place the facial tissue in the center of the design square. Make a quick sweeping stroke from the inside of the design outward to the edge and off the paper (7). Repeat the stroke, going around the entire design (8). Do not stroke the same place twice.

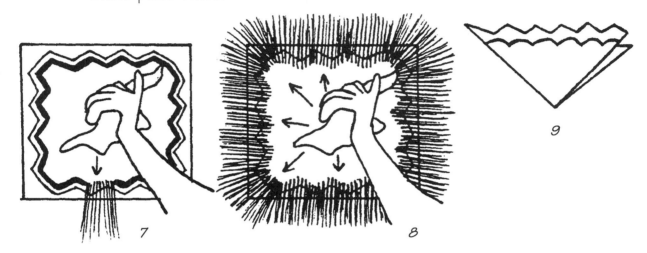

7

8

9

6. Fold the paper with the design. Draw a new design approximately 1/2" lower than the previous design (9). Draw *inside* the design you previously drew.

7. Repeat steps 2, 3, 4, 5, and 6 until the paper is too small to cut a design from. The center may be left white (10). Make sure each design is different. When the tissue is soiled, use a new one. Use a different color (darkest to lightest) on each new design.

8. Ask an adult to spray the design with a fixative.

10

So just stand back and say, "Gesundheit"!

Rainbow Wash

Materials

Each Child Needs:
- ○ 9" x 12" piece of manila art paper
- ○ 1 ditto master, or carbon paper and second sheet of manila paper
- ○ crayons
- ○ pencil
- ○ large container
- ○ water
- ○ newspaper

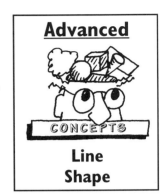

Advanced

CONCEPTS

**Line
Shape**

Directions

Have the children:

1. On the manila paper, draw a simple rainbow with clouds. Use the full sheet of paper (1).

2. Place the ditto master under the art paper. Make sure that both the picture and the purple side of the ditto master are facing up (2).

3. Trace over the lines of the rainbow. Press hard (3). The ditto will transfer the rainbow to the back of the art paper.

1

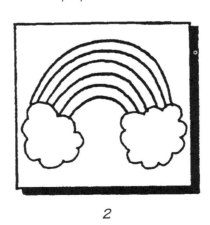

2

3

4. Turn over the art paper. You will now use the side with the dittoed lines. With crayons, color the clouds and sections of the rainbow.

Important: Do not color within 1/8" of the ditto line or the line will smear (4). Color the entire rainbow darkly (5). Colors appear in a rainbow in this order: red, yellow, green, blue, and violet.

From *Adventures with Art*, published by GoodYearBooks. Copyright © 1993 Sarah Jenkins and Margaret Foote.

Over the rainbow, Art's hoping to find

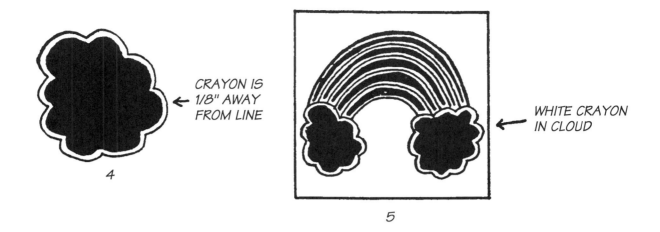

CRAYON IS
1/8" AWAY
FROM LINE
←

4

WHITE CRAYON
IN CLOUD
←

5

5. Submerge the art paper in water for approximately 15 seconds. While the paper is in water, move the paper around. The ditto line will bleed into the art paper. The crayon sections will resist the ditto (6).

6. Let the paper dry on a flat area covered with newspaper.

6

A pot of gold and some peace of mind.

Landscape and Light

Materials

Each Child Needs:
- ◯ 12" x 18" piece of white drawing paper
- ◯ pencil
- ◯ crayons

Advanced

CONCEPTS

**Perspective
Color
Design**

Directions

Note: Demonstrate each of the following steps on the board as the class moves through the project. Also, as the class begins step 7, review the concept behind light sources and shadows.

Have the children:

1. Fold the paper in half the short way. Unfold.

2. Using a pencil, lightly draw the horizon line above or below the middle of the paper (the fold) (1). Putting the horizon line above the middle will give the picture more land. Putting the line below the middle gives the picture more sky.

3. Above the horizon line, draw a range of mountains that stretch the width of the paper (2).

4. Add a row of bushes at the base of the mountains, and add three clouds in the sky. This completes the background (3). (Remember: Objects at a distance have very little detail; as you get closer to them, you see more detail.)

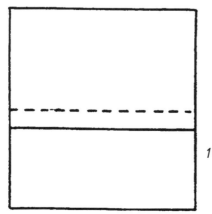

1

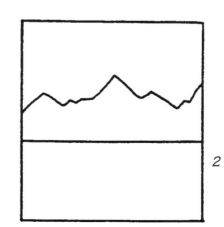

2

From *Adventures with Art*, published by GoodYearBooks. Copyright © 1993 Sarah Jenkins and Margaret Foote.

Painting a landscape is quite a delight,

5. Place a tree in the foreground with the base about an inch from the bottom of the paper. Extend it to the top of the paper. (Remember: The tree should be off-center to create balance in the composition.)

6. Place clumps of grass randomly in the foreground (4).

7. Lightly place an X in the top corner of the picture to show where the source of light is coming from. Then in pencil, lightly place shadows on the clouds, bushes, mountains, and tree (5).

8. Color the picture, keeping in mind the rules of shading (6).

9. Add a river, if desired. Display the pictures in the classroom. Note the differences in the pictures, even though everyone made the same project. Notice how everyone's unique style comes out in his or her picture.

3

4

5

6

Now if only he can get the perspective right.

91

SPRING

String-Alongs

Materials

Each Child Needs:
- ○ 8" x 11" piece of white drawing paper
- ○ 24" piece of string
- ○ 9" x 12" piece of colored art paper
- ○ tempera paint
- ○ black crayon or thin black marker
- ○ glue
- ○ containers
- ○ newspaper
- ○ heavy book

Intermediate

CONCEPTS

Line
Color

Directions

Before getting started, cover the work area with newspaper. Mix several colors of the tempera, and hand out the art paper.

Then, have the children:

1. Fold the 8" x 11" piece of paper in half. Then unfold it (1).

2. Dip half of the string in one color of paint. Then dip the second half in another color (2).

3. Lay the string in an interesting pattern on one half of the unfolded paper. Make sure the two ends of the string extend off the end of the paper together (3).

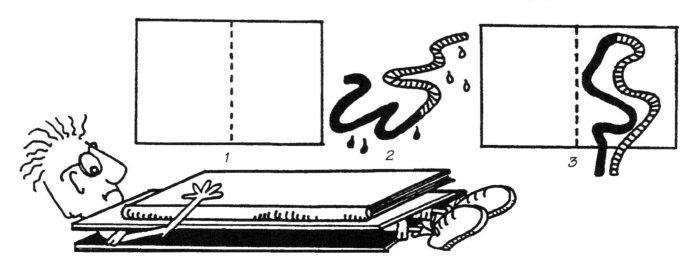

1   2   3

From *Adventures with Art*, published by GoodYearBooks. Copyright © 1993 Sarah Jenkins and Margaret Foote.

Duplicating Art is easy to do,

4. Refold the paper over string. Place the book on top of the paper. While pressing down with one hand, pull both ends of the string straight out from between the paper (4).

5. Unfold the paper and let the design dry (5).

6. Using the black crayon or marker, add detail to the design (6). Then mat the picture using a piece of paper that brings out the main colors (6).

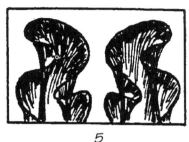
5

4

6

Suggestions

For a variation, follow steps 1 to 5. Then cut on the fold using a paper cutter. Place the bottom of both papers together, matching the design. Perform step 6. Your design might look like this (7):

7

But what in the world would we do with two?

Dual Designs

Materials

Each Child Needs:
- ○ 9" x 12" piece of art paper
- ○ two 9" x 12" pieces of oaktag
- ○ old toothbrush
- ○ tempera paint and containers
- ○ scissors
- ○ newspaper
- ○ pencil
- ○ thin black marker

Advanced

CONCEPTS

**Texture
Line**

Directions

Before getting started, cover the work area with newspaper. Mix a container of green paint and a container of orange paint to a thin consistency. Hand out the art paper and oaktag to the children.

Then, have the children:

1. Fold the art paper and one sheet of oaktag in half the short way. Unfold.
2. On the oaktag, draw the outline of three carrots, starting at the fold and extending down on the bottom half of the paper. Just draw the carrots, not their greens (1).
3. On the top half of the same sheet, draw the outline of the carrot greens, making sure the bottom of the leaves touch the top of the carrots, meeting at the fold (1).
4. Cut the oaktag in half along the fold. Cut out the carrots and greens. You now have two separate stencils.
5. Place the extra piece of oaktag (9" x 12") over the top half of the folded art paper. This oaktag will be used to protect the paper from paint splatters. Place the carrot stencil on the bottom half of the art paper (2).
6. Dip the toothbrush into the orange paint. Point the bristles down, and run your fingers along them. This will create a splattering effect on the paper. Continue splattering until the carrots look the way you want them to. (Be careful not to splatter anyone!)

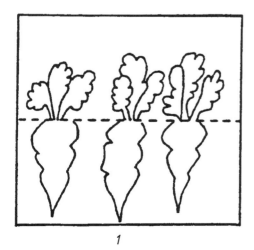

1

From *Adventures with Art*, published by GoodYearBooks. Copyright © 1993 Sarah Jenkins and Margaret Foote.

Art enjoys painting, but he's not very neat,

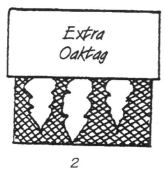

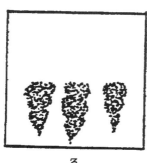

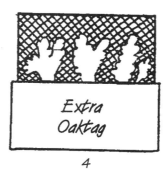

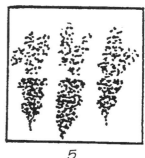

2   3   4   5

7. Take the stencil off the art paper and let the carrots dry (3). Wash the toothbrush thoroughly.

8. Place the extra oaktag over the bottom half of the art paper, covering the carrots. Place the "carrot greens" stencil over the top half of the art paper (4). Line up the stencil with the painted carrots.

9. Repeat step 6 using green paint. Remove the stencil and let the paint dry (5).

10. Using a black marker, add details to the carrots and their greens (6). Mat the picture using orange paper.

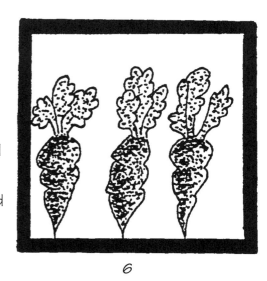

6

Suggestions

For a variation, paint two separate objects on the top and bottom of the art paper. Use different colors for each object (7).

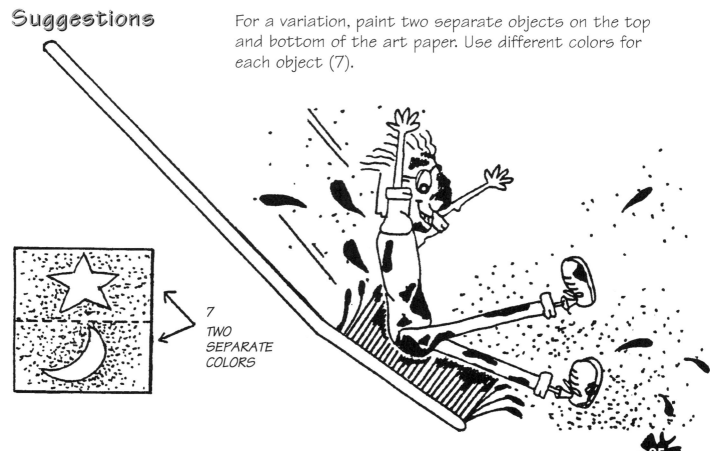

7

TWO SEPARATE COLORS

In fact, staying clean would be quite a feat.

Leafy Stencils

Materials

Easy

CONCEPTS

Design Textures

Each Child Needs:
- ○ white or black art paper cut in large circles
- ○ several colors of tempera paint
- ○ paintbrushes or roller
- ○ newspaper
- ○ fresh green leaves in various sizes

Directions

Before getting started, cover the work area with newspaper.

Then, have the children:

1. Select a leaf from the batch. Place the leaf on the newspaper. Dip the paintbrush in the paint and then cover the back of the leaf with one color (1).

2. Set the leaf aside on a clean sheet of newspaper. Lay the art paper on top of the leaf (2). Rub the leaf on the paper with your fingers (make sure you rub the entire paper).

1

2

From *Adventures with Art*, published by GoodYearBooks. Copyright © 1993 Sarah Jenkins and Margaret Foote.

96

SPRING

Art painted a picture and now you see,